HAVE YOU SEEN
CHRISTMAS?

by Vicki Howie

Illustrated by Caroline Pedler

Christmas Eve dawned cold and gray over the city.
A bitter wind shook the Christmas lights that were strung across High Street and sent paper cups rolling along the sidewalk.

It swirled snow like white confetti around the steeples of city churches and it picked up newspapers and flattened them against colorful shop windows.

In the sheltered doorway of a department store, a small scruffy dog named "Christmas" sniffed the cold air with interest and went in search of something to eat.

The dog left his young master fast asleep, huddled inside his sleeping bag.

There he stayed until the first shoppers disturbed him and
he awoke to find his only companion gone.

Just around the corner, Benny and Mia were enjoying the Christmas holidays, playing hide-and-seek around their parents' fruit and vegetable stall. Apples, cranberries, oranges and grapes glistened with wet snow under the striped awning.

"Come out! I can see you!" shouted Benny. Mia's hat bobbed up from behind a box full of oranges.

"Hey, Dad!" she cried. "Why do you need so many oranges?"

"You'll see!" he replied, mysteriously. "Now why don't you two get out from under my feet. It's going to be a busy day.

"Go and find your friend, Luke. I think I saw him in a doorway by the bus stop."

"OK!" said Benny. "Then we can see Christmas, his funny little dog. I *love* that dog!"

Benny and Mia set off toward the main road.

They waved to Jamie, who was just coming out of the church hall.

"Why does Luke live on the street?" asked Mia. "Doesn't he have a home like us?"

"No, Luke is homeless. It is very sad," explained Benny. "He came to the city hoping to find a job, but it was more difficult than he thought."

"At least he's got his dog," said Mia.

Benny nodded.

"Luke got him at the animal rescue center. Someone bought him for Christmas and then couldn't take care of him."

"I wish he was *my* dog," said Mia. "He's the friendliest dog in the world!"

Rounding the corner, Benny and Mia saw Luke. He was slouched against a shop window, holding his head in his hands.

"What's the matter, Luke?"

Luke turned his pale face toward them.

"It's my dog!" he explained. "Christmas is missing. He's never left my side before now."

"Oh, no!" The children stared at one another in dismay.

"Why don't you look for him?" suggested Mia.

Luke shook his head.

"He might come back while I am out looking for him."

"Don't worry, Luke!" said Benny. "We'll go and look for your dog. We'll bring him back—just you wait and see!"

Benny and Mia began to run along the sidewalk and almost collided with a lady coming out of the department store. She dropped several bags and bent to pick them up.

"Sorry!" exclaimed Mia. "But we're looking for Christmas. Have *you* seen Christmas?"

"Have I seen Christmas?" repeated the lady. "I should think so! Christmas is in there!" She pointed into the busy store.

"Oh, thank you!" chorused the children.

They went in through the heavy glass doors and found themselves among counters displaying handbags, scarfs and gloves.

"I can't see Christmas," said Benny, bending down and looking between the feet of all the shoppers. "Perhaps he's gone up to the toy department."

At the top of the escalator, the children pushed their way through crowds gathered around their favorite toys. Two children were arguing over a robot.

"I saw it first!" said one, pulling at the legs.

"Dad said *I* could have it," yelled the other, tugging at its head.

"Put it back, both of you!" ordered their father, his face bright red with annoyance.

"Come on, Mia!" said Benny, taking her hand. "Christmas obviously isn't here. Let's go back outside!"

A security guard was standing in the shop doorway.

"Excuse me!" said Benny boldly.

"We're looking for Christmas. Have *you* seen Christmas?"

"Well now," said the man, scratching his head, "have you been down to the City Square? I'd say Christmas was there!"

The children ran on along the sidewalk. Their warm breath hung in the air like tiny snow clouds.

Turning the corner into the Square, they gasped at the sight of a tall Christmas tree lit with hundreds of Christmas lights. Underneath it, children skated on a gleaming ice-rink. They whirled and twirled, criss-crossing the ice as dance music blared from a loudspeaker.

"Wow! That's beautiful!" said Mia, her eyes sparkling.

"But I still can't see Christmas!" said Benny. "And we'll have to go back soon. Luke will be waiting for us."

They retraced their steps along the crowded sidewalk, wondering what they would say to Luke. Above their heads, the star decorations on the lamp posts flickered and burst into light. When they were nearly back to Luke's doorway, they saw that Jamie had stopped to talk to him.

"Jamie!" cried the children, running up to him. "We've been looking and looking but we can't find Christmas anywhere."

"I see," said Jamie gravely. "So Christmas has gone

missing. Well, I think I might know where we could find
Christmas. Come with me."

Luke got to his feet and followed the puzzled children into
the adjoining street and down the steps that led to the hall
under the church.

As they opened the door, light and warmth flooded out and
a delicious smell of hot sausages wafted under their noses.
Men and women of all ages, dressed in old coats, jumpers,
and shawls, sat at a long table decorated with bowls of

oranges. They were eating steaming plates of food served by
a team of church helpers.

And *under* the table, his ears pricked up and his tail
thumping the floor, sat a small scruffy dog, a sausage poking
out of the corner of his mouth.

"There's Christmas!" shouted Luke, running in out of the
cold to give him a hug. "Jamie was right."

Later, Jamie lit the candles and invited everyone to crowd around a beautiful Nativity set.

"At the first Christmas," began Jamie, "there was nowhere for Mary and Joseph to stay in Bethlehem. They were homeless. The streets were bustling full of people who had traveled there for the census. No one had time for them. There was no room for them at the inn. But Jesus was born in a stable because the innkeeper tried to help them.

"Please stay now as long as you like. There will be hot drinks for everyone and Christmas lunch will be provided tomorrow."

People started to clean up.

"Come home with us for Christmas," Benny said to Luke. "I know Dad wouldn't mind. There are always enough vegetables to eat!"

"Oh, yes!" said Mia. "Then Christmas can come to our house too!"

Luke walked with them in silence through the falling snow. "I found Christmas today," he said after a while. "I was cold and hungry and miserable, but the people in the church gave me dry, warm clothes and hot food to eat. I lost my dog and had nowhere to go, but you helped me find him and are letting me come home with you. You've all made me feel that someone cares about me. We were all looking for Christmas—but it's right here!"

Benny thought about the store full of people and the children arguing over the toys. Mia thought about the snowy

scene and the tree with all its lights. Luke was right.

And Christmas, the small scruffy dog who liked sausages, barked and wagged his tail.

Published in the United States of America by
Abingdon Press, 201 Eighth Avenue South,
Nashville, Tennessee 37202

ISBN 0-687-49678-0

First edition 2006

Editorial Director Annette Reynolds
Editor Nicola Bull
Art Director Gerald Rogers
Pre-production Krystyna Kowalska Hewitt
Production John Laister

Printed and bound in Singapore